GUIDING CHILDREN THROUGH THE SOCIAL STUDIES

AUTHORS

Robert W. Reynolds, *Committee Chairman,* Consultant, Elementary Education, California State Department of Education

Dorothea Cox, Coordinator, Curriculum, San Mateo County Schools

Archie Edwards, Principal, Pacific Elementary School, Highland Elementary School District

Helen Heffernan, Chief, Bureau of Elementary Education, California State Department of Education

Mrs. Margaret Lenz, Consultant, Curriculum, Rialto Elementary School District

John U. Michaelis, Professor, Education, University of California

Penrod Moss, Director, Curriculum, Dixie Elementary School District

Lucile M. Nixon, Consultant, Elementary Education, Palo Alto City Unified Schools

Mrs. Iola Threatt, Teacher, Mission Elementary School, Mission Elementary School District

Copyright 1964

National Education Association of the United States
Department of Elementary-Kindergarten-Nursery Education

Library of Congress Catalog Number 64-17469

Single copy, $1. Discounts on quantity orders: 10 percent on
2-9 copies and 20 percent on 10 or more copies. All orders
which amount to $2 or less must be accompanied by pay-
ment. Shipping is charged on all orders not paid for in ad-
vance. Order from and make checks payable to the National
Education Association, 1201 Sixteenth Street, N.W., Washington, D.C. 20036.

CONTENTS

INTRODUCTION

The place of the social studies in any era is to give coherence to the study of one's cultural heritage, to provide mental anchorage in a world that appears to grow increasingly more complex during each new generation. In the social studies, it is possible for pupils to find coherence, continuity, and insight into the basic nature of human endeavors and the persistent problems which beset mankind.

This bulletin presents a perspective for the social studies which is designed to enable teachers to discern coherence, continuity, and preciseness in the study of human affairs.

Chapter I presents the view that the vast majority of problems that beset mankind today are those in which solutions can be achieved only through the creative efforts of the social scientists in the context of a social order which strives to bring about harmonious living conditions for all its citizens.

Studies of history and geography in the traditional connotation of the terms are not enough to equip modern day youth with the necessary understandings, incentives, and skills for solving the problems facing any society, now or in the future. The solutions are inherent in the understandings within each of the social sciences comprising the social studies and in a broad understanding of the interrelationships of knowledges among the social sciences.

In our designs to develop social studies programs, we must be concerned with more than the structure of content in history, geography, economics, political science, anthropology, sociology, and philosophy. We must establish clearly the relatedness of the studies to the social needs of our times, to the values to which our society is committed, to the nature of the learner, and to effective strategies for learning. The social studies must be so taught that children acquire practiced skill in the democratic processes; it must evolve such faith in human nature, democracy, and the possibility of progress through intelligent cooperation that it becomes deeply rooted in the behavior of each pupil.

Chapter II presents the view that the social studies is a dynamic area of the curriculum in which pupils engage in the investigation of cultural forms and processes in a laboratory setting.

The affairs of mankind viewed at any one level of society are perceived as having a parallel at any other level. Thus, an issue over property rights in the sandbox of the kindergarten or in the sharing of tools during construction in the first grade is viewed as having relatedness to issues among siblings at home, to a conflict over water rights at the state level, or to colonization at the national or international level. A task of the teacher is to seek ways for pupils to relate data to personal example and then set about purposely to lift the example to ever higher levels of abstraction.

A multidisciplinary treatment of the study of cultures is necessary in order to comprehend the wide variations among cultures. Seeking an understanding of contrasting modes of living draws on the knowledge and skills refined and organized into the various social science fields. Major generalizations from the social sciences useful as organizing centers for relating facts and other information are identified.

Rather than organize the learning activities to teach generalizations from the social sciences on a subject-matter-to-be-learned approach, the view is taken that generalizations are to be viewed as large central ideas around which facts and other information have relatedness. This approach retains the cohesive structure of the culture being studied and stresses analysis and categorization of raw data in terms of concepts, generalizations, and categories of knowledge.

Stress is given to the inductive processes for developing major generalizations as characteristics of a laboratory subject. The starting point is with the identification by pupils of related pieces of information and then organization of the pieces in such ways that the relatedness of the raw data to one or more significant ideas from the social sciences becomes apparent.

Descriptions of learning activities showing relatedness of teacher purpose to pupil purpose, pupil purpose to learning activities, learning activities to the accumulation of related sets of facts, specific facts to concepts, concepts to subgeneralizations, and subgeneralizations to major generalizations from the social sciences are presented.

Chapter III presents the view that instruction for children in the primary grades must take into consideration the new knowledge about child growth and development, the subject matter to be learned, and the processes through which pupils make the subject matter of the school a part of themselves.

Utilizing a frame of reference centering on characteristics of children as they are, as they grow, and what they become through the educative processes, the authors offer insight into procedures for moving pupils toward comprehension of major concepts and generalizations about citizenship, democracy, knowledge, and social change.

For many children, the local environment is less familiar than places a considerable distance from home. Although pupils in the primary years are more informed in matters of human affairs than earlier generations, superficial knowledge is not enough to develop the major understandings and skills required for effective performance in modern society. Inquiry must move beyond the mere gathering of description to the identification of factors that operate to bring about cultural similarities and differences. Descriptions of ways in which pupils are provided opportunities to examine significant elements of culture through more than one perspective are presented. Examples of ways in which pupils learn to hypothesize and develop ideas and to check their hypotheses and ideas through application as well as through verbalization are described.

Chapter IV presents the view of the social studies program in the intermediate grades as a laboratory field for the study of cultural forms and processes. Stress is given to the use of inductive processes for learning and to the utilization of primary sources of information. Emphases include developing and practicing techniques and skills of inquiry, analyzing cultural patterns, and reshaping facts and other information in ways that enable pupils to generalize and categorize data in terms of major ideas from the social sciences. The view is taken that generalizations evolved by pupils are to be converted by them into hypotheses for further investigation of contrasting cultural patterns.

The myriad of facts and other information acquired by pupils through the years, which may appear to them to be unrelated, can be brought together in a meaningful manner. Through guidance, pupils discover relatedness among the school's subject matters to personal interests, aspirations, and activities; to problems and other concerns of peers, friends, family, and society in general; and to fundamental ideas about mankind. The social studies can then become for pupils and teachers a sensible, feasible, and socially useful area of the total school curriculum.

Descriptions of learning activities showing the analysis of learning outcomes in relationship to teacher and pupil purposes and to facts, concepts, and generalizations offer a perspective useful to teachers both in making social studies meaningful for pupils, parents, and their own purposes and in planning learning activities in the intermediate grades.

CHAPTER I

Reasons for Teaching the SOCIAL STUDIES

As the word *science* is generally used, the meaning is usually limited to the physical sciences. No one will question the tremendous progress that has been made in the physical sciences in the twentieth century. The scientist has been able to carry on extensive experimentation in order to wrest hitherto hidden secrets from nature. Furthermore, he has been able to reduce his findings to mathematical terms. The very precision and exactitude of findings in the physical sciences have been the source of feelings of security to people living daily with the uncertainties of our anxious age.

Science in its broadest meaning, however, is not limited to the physical sciences. Ascending the scale of the various sciences, progress in the life sciences becomes more difficult. Experimentation and expression of findings in quantitative terms present difficulties because the life scientist encounters more variables dealing with living organisms than the physi-

cal scientist does dealing with matter and energy. However, progress in the life sciences has been accelerated as the life scientist has been able to use certain techniques of quantitative analysis perfected by the physical scientist.

Most difficult of all the sciences are the social sciences which deal not only with man and all his complex behaviors but also with man in relation to his natural environment, with man as he functions in a wide variety of social groups, with the interrelations between and among social groups, and with the complex domestic, economic, political, vocational, religious, and aesthetic institutions and organizations man has developed to order and control these relationships.

Socially minded citizens recognize the importance of the social sciences. None will question that each and all of the social sciences are involved in a transition to a peaceful world in which man's resources can be constructively employed in the advancement of civilization. Each one will affirm that the curriculum of the school must provide the American electorate with knowledge of the social sciences basic to intelligent decision.

Funds have been available for limitless research in the physical sciences. We know now that man can reach the moon because the problems posed by such an adventure can be solved experimentally and charted mathematically.

We are beginning to spend more funds on the life sciences. The potential rewards of such expenditures can be measured in increased productivity, in the conquest of disease, and in the prolongation of human life. These materialistic gains have an appeal and result in more liberal allocations from the government as well as from the foundations.

But the social sciences in which man's major problems exist have not aroused similar determination to carry on essential research leading to their solution. We do not seem much closer to the solution of our most vexing domestic and international problems than we were 20 or 30 years ago. Decisions in the field of the social sciences are frequently left to persons with sufficient political and financial resources to get themselves elected to public office but whose knowledge of the social sciences is most elementary and frequently erroneous or contrary to democratic principles.

In spite of the progress in the physical sciences, we are unable to use what the scientists have discovered because we have lagged in the social sciences. Perhaps enough has been said to make the point that the creative energies of social scientists should be directed to research designed to find solutions to our most pressing domestic and international problems rather than to maintenance of an intolerable status quo.

Studies of history and geography alone are not enough to equip modern day youth with the necessary understandings, incentives, and skills for solving the problems facing any society, now or in the future. The solutions are inherent in the understandings within each of the eight social sciences (p. 25) and in a broad understanding of the interrelationships among the social sciences. Social scientists recognize the importance of interrelationships:

A historian has stated: "It is the proper scope of history to remind us perpetually that no one discipline can present an orderly view of man and society." [1]

A geographer has stressed the idea that "geography examines the relationships not only between man and his habitat, but also between man and the various cultural features resulting from economic, social or political processes." [2]

An economist has pointed out that "there is cross-fertilization, at levels both of process and content, between economics and other disciplines that are concerned with human behavior and which carry on their work in the scientific tradition." [3]

An anthropologist has defined anthropology as "the generalizing science about all varieties and all aspects of mankind." [4]

A sociologist has stated that "the student should have an integrated view of society, of social processes, no matter how elementary this view may be. Only thus can a student gain an idea of a science of society as a coherent body of thought." [5]

Pupils approaching the study of a region, such as sub-Sahara Africa, or a culture, such as Japan, or a study showing the development of a problem, such as conservation of our natural resources, must utilize knowledge from many of the social sciences to acquire genuine understanding. As area specialists have indicated, attention must be given to the

---

[1] National Education Association, Project on Instruction. *The Scholars Look at the Schools.* Washington, D.C.: the Association, 1962. p. 41.

[2] *Ibid.,* p. 39.

[3] American Council of Learned Societies and the National Council for the Social Studies, a department of the National Education Association. *The Social Studies and the Social Sciences.* New York: Harcourt, Brace and World, 1962. p. 49.

[4] *Ibid.,* p. 132.

[5] *Ibid.,* p. 141.

influence of geography, the history of the people, the ways people have met their basic human needs for food, clothing, shelter, communication, transportation, education, and religious and aesthetic expression.[6] Seeking pertinent facts from the many social sciences has helped learners see relationships and develop crosscultural understandings—an outcome stressed by scholars in the social sciences. Modern perceptual psychologists tell us that learning is a problem of an individual's personal discovery of meaning. He discovers meaning as he becomes increasingly aware of relationships.

In the constant reconstruction of curriculum, teachers, supervisors, curriculum consultants, administrators, and persons engaged in the professional preparation of educators are simultaneously working on five basic considerations. They are studying—

1. The social needs of our times.
2. The values to which our society is committed.
3. The nature of the learner.
4. The nature of the learning process.
5. The structure of the content to be learned.

The Social Needs of Our Times. At any time and under any conditions, children need to learn as much as they can about the world in which they live in order that they may relate themselves to it, may contribute to its welfare, and may participate intelligently in its improvement. In speaking of the purposes of the social studies, Preston E. James, professor of geography at Syracuse University, has stated:

> It is expected that they [the social sciences] will provide perspective regarding the diverse conditions of the modern world.[7]

In our contemporary world, schools must provide a broad curriculum suited to the maturity of children which will acquaint them with the world in which they live and the problems with which it is presently confronted.

Important as is knowledge, it is not enough. Dr. Strayer, professor of history at Princeton University, has stated:

> . . . the social studies are supposed to inculcate certain attitudes and skills. The desired attitudes include respect for evidence even when it goes against prejudices and preconceptions, tolerance for differing points of view, appreciation of human dignity, a sense of civic responsibility and devotion to country. The skills are those associated with the analysis and solution of social problems: ability to discover relevant facts, to organize facts into meaningful patterns, to weigh conflicting evidence and discount biased statements, and to choose among various interpretations and policies.[8]

The teacher has the responsibility to develop strong interests in humanity and attitudes of concern for the welfare of all human beings. Along with enlightened intelligence, social studies must be so taught that children have faith in human nature, in democracy, and in the possibility of progress through intelligent cooperation. The teacher also has the responsibility to liberate children from unwarranted prejudice and provincialism, from acceptance of superficial opinion and unproved beliefs, and from complacency and smug individualism.

We note in contemporary society a tendency to retreat into privatism. This kind of thinking can be disastrous to democracy. The great social need of our times is a feeling of personal responsibility; otherwise, we become prey to selfish and unscrupulous manipulators who exploit the unthinking person for his personal and often antisocial ends.

At the meeting of the American Association of School Administrators held in Atlantic City in February 1962, Dr. Ralph Bunche said:

> . . . in assessing future prospects for peace and human well-being much more importance attaches to the individual, to individual attitudes and responsibilities, than to institutions or mechanisms; for the greatest obstacle to peace in the world takes shape in the towering walls of distrust which block true communications

---

[6] See: American Council of Learned Societies and the National Council for the Social Studies, a department of the National Education Association. *The Social Studies and the Social Sciences.* New York: Harcourt, Brace and World, 1962. pp. 191-281.

[7] *Ibid.,* p. 44.

[8] *Ibid.,* p. 23.

between man and man, people and people, government and government.

The Values to Which Our Society Is Committed. As Dr. Norton E. Long, professor of political science at Northwestern University, has stated:

> No society worthy of survival will fail to fight to defend its values. The political values of our society are in need of defense, not only from attack from without and within, but from the far more deadly enemy of neglect and lack of understanding on the part of those who nominally adhere to them.[9]

Current writers on education usually note that new values are emerging and frequently do not specify what these new values actually are. For nearly 200 years, our country has had a moral commitment to the values of democracy. Perhaps it is an oversimplification to say that the major values of democracy can be incorporated in three statements:

1. Ability and willingness to seek the facts (truth) and courage to act unfailingly in terms of these facts or this truth

2. Regard for the rights and sanctity of human personality

3. Moral integrity or willingness to live by the values one has accepted to live by. This would certainly include individual responsibility and condemn any retreat into privatism.

But these emerging new values are still intriguing. Alva Myrdal, who collaborated with her husband Gunnar Myrdal on *Crisis in the Population Problem,* writes of the emerging values in these words:

> What we need for our future development is not more artifacts, more material goods. What we seem to need is a much more explicit goal for the future, to endow life with richer experiences, to deal with constantly better qualities. . . .
>
> It is in these new directions—of truly serving our fellow men, enjoying our leisure in a culturally richer way, deepening our sensitivity and heightening our creativity—that we find our values moving. And it is in these directions that we can push on to even more glorious conquests.[10]

Recall again the basic values of democracy—truth, regard for human personality, moral integrity—and nothing incompatible exists between these values and the modern directions perceived by Mrs. Myrdal. Her new directions are in truth the outcome of lives well lived in terms of the basic values to which our society must always have a moral commitment or must forsake democracy as a way of life.

The social studies make unique and direct contributions to such basic societal goals as truth, regard for mankind, and moral integrity. These are prerequisites for self-realization, human relationships, civic competence, economic efficiency, and thinking ability. Of central importance are the contributions that the social studies make to the development of responsible citizenship which includes the thinking processes, concepts, understandings, attitudes, appreciations, and skills essential to learning and living in our times.

The Nature of the Learner. During the twentieth century, psychology has made many significant contributions to education. The most significant has been the building up of mountains of evidence that individuals differ from one another in every conceivable way and that no amount of grouping can ever produce a group of people sufficiently alike so they will all respond identically to teaching stimuli.

For education generally and for social studies particularly, this means that any learning experience must provide a wide range of interests, utilize a wide variety of instructional materials, and provide for many types of firsthand and vicarious experiences. With the guidance of a teacher skillful in organization, a program highly individualized to the needs of each child can be provided; and opportunity for sharing each child's discoveries can be found in group discussion.

Although children differ greatly from one another, all pass through a developmental sequence that can be roughly

---

[9] *Ibid.,* p. 92.

[10] Myrdal, Alva. "The Power of Education." *Education in World Perspective.* (Edited by Emmet John Hughes.) New York: Harper & Row, 1962. p. 159.

described in terms of chronological age. Within a year or two, nearly all children will show comparable developmental characteristics. They won't all walk at the same time; their teeth will not erupt at the same time; they will not all talk at the same time; they will not all develop the same degree of muscular coordination at the same time. Every family with more than one child can attest to these statements. But just as the timing of these developmental characteristics differs, by the same token, all children will not read at the same time; all children will not develop the ability to carry a tune at the same time; all children will not acquire basic social studies or scientific concepts at the same time. The problem of the teacher and the curriculum maker is to be aware of the nature of the learner and create situations in which each can learn at his own rate, pursue his interests, work with large and small groups in activities designed to develop concepts, and have many experiences free from feelings of fear, frustration, or inadequacy.

The Nature of the Learning Process. A tremendous amount of material on learning theory is currently being produced. Even a superficial analysis of the assumptions educational psychologists are now attempting to establish by research would consume many hours.

More profitable would be an attempt to point out what learning theories may provide directives for teachers in their guidance of children's learning. Teachers need to focus attention on these questions:

1. What are the children in their groups like; what are their purposes, beliefs, values, and understandings?

2. What experiences will facilitate growth and provide opportunity for children to clarify their purposes, test their beliefs and values, and measure the degree of their understanding?

3. How does an environment, in which each child is free to be his unique, creative self and in which he can test reality in vital situations, promote growth?

4. How can one assess his own instructional methods, be willing to discard those that seem ineffective, and experiment with techniques to which pupils seem more responsive?

5. Is experience essential to any real learning? The learner must have past experience to put into his reading or he cannot read with meaning. Actually, one can read only what he already knows. Experience must precede reading, looking at motion pictures, or using any of the self-instructional materials currently becoming available.

6. Does learning go on all the time? The teacher helps determine the rate, direction, and quality of learning by the variety and vitality of experiences provided.

No area of study will prove more rewarding to the teacher than that of modern learning theory. This constitutes the professional heart of the teacher's task, and here again educators are confronted with an explosion of knowledge.

On the basis of recent findings related to learning theory, the use of dynamic techniques of instruction is being emphasized. It is widely recognized that a dynamic, active program of instruction is needed in which children can discover key concepts and formulate generalizations. Memorization of isolated facts is vehemently condemned by the scholars in the disciplines as well as by educational leaders. At the same time, the importance of adequate and reliable information for use in concept development is fully recognized.

Fundamental to the emphasis on dynamic and active methods of instruction appear to be certain concepts about children and how they learn. For example, children's curiosity, desire to investigate, urge to communicate, need to express themselves creatively, and ability to conceptualize ideas appear to be important elements in current thinking and learning. Readiness for learning is being viewed more in the context of meaningfulness of instruction than in the context of states of maturation. The importance of problem solving as a means of discovering concepts, formulating generalizations, and developing scientific attitudes and skills is becoming increasingly apparent. Concern about organizing knowledge into a meaningful structure of broad applicability is indicative of the shift in emphasis from specific notions of transfer of learning to more general notions of transfer. Self-actualization, self-esteem, and a wholesome self-concept appear to be of prime importance in learning in the social studies as well as in the process of socialization.[11]

Scientific approaches to study and problem solving are being stressed, and direct attention is being given to the utilization of modes of inquiry employed by social scientists. It is believed that in addition to improving learning and making it more exciting, children will begin to develop greater insight into methods of investigation used by social scientists. In addition to stressing general scientific approaches in which problems are defined, questions or hypotheses are stated, data are gathered and evaluated, and interpretations and conclusions are drawn, attention is being given to specific modes of inquiry. Among these are mapping, doing field studies, making careful observations, recording data, role playing, interviewing, experimenting, analyzing issues, considering consequences of different courses of action, analyzing realia, appraising various sources of information, and applying criteria to proposals and actions. It is clear that direct experience in using such techniques is essential to the achievement of the goals of the social studies.

Among other methods being emphasized are techniques for making crosscultural comparisons. Of primary importance is the provision of units of instruction that deal fully with groups under study. As differences are discovered, it is recommended that a search be made for the reasons why differences exist. This leads children to discover again and again the impact of culture upon ways of living and thus contributes to a growing *concept of culture*. Coupled with emphasis on the culture concept is attention to basic social processes that operate in all cultures and to processes of change that may be discovered in many different units of instruction. For example, how people make decisions in light of their values, how interaction with others contributes to change, how interaction with the physical environment influences people's ways of living—all these are brought together and illuminated as comparisons are made.

The Structure of the Content To Be Learned. The structure for the social studies is composed of the social sciences that serve as the source of key ideas, concepts, generalizations, and modes of inquiry for emphasis in the social studies program. To neglect this element or any one of the other basic considerations identified previously (the social needs of our times, the values to which our society is committed, the nature of the learner, and the nature of the learning process) is to create an imbalance in curriculum planning that can result only in a lowering of the quality of instruction. If such basic values as respect for the individual, concern for general welfare, and use of rational thinking to solve problems are neglected, how can children develop the attitudes, appreciations, and understandings essential to living in our times? If inadequate attention is given to children's cultural backgrounds, thinking processes, basic urges and drives, individual differences, and needs to discover, create, and communicate with others, how can maximum learning be achieved on the part of each child? If key concepts, main ideas, and methods of investigation from the social sciences are overlooked, how can children develop the understandings, skills, and attitudes needed to deal with human relationships and to solve social problems?

As a political scientist recently pointed out and as leading educators have stressed for many years, basic attitudes and concepts are formed early in the lives of children:

> Children in the elementary grades develop strong, positive feelings toward obeying the laws. They also attach strong feelings to democratic ideals, such as freedom and civic responsibility, duties, and rights. They believe people should be interested in politics, and by third grade they are able and ready to express a party identification.[12]

---

[11] See: Association for Supervision and Curriculum Development. *Perceiving, Behaving, Becoming.* 1962 Yearbook. Washington, D.C.: the Association, a department of the National Education Association, 1962.

[12] National Education Association, Project on Instruction. *The Scholars Look at the Schools.* Washington, D.C.: the Association, 1962. p. 41.

Similar statements can be made about attitudes and concepts in other areas of learning. The fundamental implication is that the social studies in the early grades must be planned to initiate the development of those basic attitudes, concepts, and skills that are of central importance in our way of life. In no instance should incidental approaches take the place of a well-designed program of instruction geared to the potentialities of young children.

As units of instruction are planned to take children far beyond their own communities, effort should be made to build the foundations of meaning and understanding that are needed to make crosscultural comparisons and to understand the ways of living of others. Concepts of interdependence, culture, change, time, distance, direction, and the like must be developed in the context of units on the home, neighborhood, and community so that they can be discovered anew in studies of ancient and modern Eastern and Western cultures. Understandable crosscultural comparisons are possible only when children have a meaningful basis for making comparisons and have developed the abilities needed to find and understand the reasons why differences exist. Concepts and ideas gained through travel, television, radio, motion pictures, and other mass media need to be clarified, interpreted, and structured so that they can be brought to bear upon the study of ways of living both here and in other places. Erroneous understandings must be corrected, and attention must be given to developing proper attitudes before socially undesirable attitudes become deeply rooted.

The program in the middle and upper grades should extend and deepen learnings attained in the early grades. New concepts and ideas should be introduced and linked to earlier learnings in ways that give increasing insight into ways of living at home and in other places. Basic generalizations involving such concepts as interdependence, culture, change, and impact of science and technology should be discovered and formulated by children in a variety of new situations. Insights into the structure of the social sciences will be achieved as concepts are attained, generalizations are formulated, and modes of inquiry are explored and put to use in meaningful learning experiences. Attitudes, beliefs, values, and behavior patterns will be strengthened as critical thinking and understanding continue to be emphasized as the bases for intelligent action. Basic skills essential to both immediate and lifelong learning will be brought to higher levels of development as a variety of materials, activities, and techniques of investigation are critically selected and made a part of the instructional program.

Strong recommendations have been made by scholars in relation to area studies that draw materials from all disciplines related to a given region. Among the areas recommended for study are Latin America, India, Africa, Asia, the Middle East, Russia, and Eastern Europe. The need to draw content from many disciplines in planning area studies has recently been highlighted by a social scientist as follows:

> Literature, music, art, physical geography, and still other subjects can each contribute to the student's knowledge of the area, and this should never be forgotten in planning a curriculum . . . [and] it is reasonable to assume that the school child will acquire his knowledge of the area largely through the social studies.[13]

As area studies are planned, teachers must avoid cramming existing instruction with more bits of information lest "something crucial be lost—the educational opportunity to see another part of the world as a whole, as an integral socio-cultural system." [14] According to a specialist on Russia and Eastern Europe, properly planned area studies have such advantages as the following: (a) a deeper understanding of self and one's own society, (b) practical knowledge about important areas of the world, (c) insight into cultural relativity, and (d) "the integration of all of the social sciences." [15]

---

[13] American Council of Learned Societies and the National Council for the Social Studies, a department of the National Education Association. *The Social Studies and the Social Sciences.* New York: Harcourt, Brace and World, 1962. pp. 242-43.

[14] *Ibid.,* p. 244.

[15] *Ibid.*

Two principles appear to be clear as we consider recommendations such as these which come from social scientists who are helping to plan social studies instruction in the schools. First, valid and meaningful relationships must be stressed within each discipline as well as among disciplines. Secondly, area studies, which sometimes are referred to by curriculum workers as culture or life studies, have an important place in the program and should be designed to give a cohesive view of the area under study. With continuing assistance from social scientists, it should be possible to achieve with increasing effectiveness the long-standing objective of curriculum workers to provide units that truly highlight significant interrelationships.

No task in education is greater than that of the educator who seriously confronts the questions of what to teach and how to teach it in the social studies because the purposes of the social studies come very close to being the purposes of all education.

Educators must take into account the myriad of changes occurring in the world today. They must help develop the mind and character of human beings who will be able to cope with these changes. We cannot possibly know what all these changes will be, so we must help children learn and use the methods used by scientifically minded persons—the methods of observation, experimentation, acquaintance with data sources, collection of pertinent data, inquiry, and problem solving. These techniques must be applied to content available now, but if the process is effectively used, the methods children learn can be applied in new situations of which our generation is not aware.

Above all, we must not fear the future for ourselves or our pupils. Great human resources are becoming increasingly available around the world. Educators need the courage to experiment not exclusively with mechanical organization that is easy and peripheral to the real problem but with methods of teaching, of individualizing instruction, of inquiry training, of exploring new and interesting content. The world needs people of imagination, humor, patience; these qualities are especially needed in working with people. The world needs integrity, courage, and a sense of personal responsibility. The social studies provide the culture medium in which these qualities can develop. The children are surrounded by these all the time; they cannot escape them.

In an information bulletin that is published by a public utilities corporation, this statement appeared which probably summarizes a wise response to the question: Dare the schools neglect the social studies? The quotation is as follows:

> The average age of the world's great civilizations has been 200 years. These civilizations progressed through this sequence:
>
>> From Bondage to Spiritual Faith
>> From Spiritual Faith to Great Courage
>> From Courage to Liberty
>> From Liberty to Abundance
>> From Abundance to Selfishness
>> From Selfishness to Complacency
>> From Complacency to Apathy
>> From Apathy to Dependence
>> From Dependence Back Again to Bondage
>
> In 14 years, the United States will be 200 years old. This cycle is not inevitable—it depends on you![16]

[16] Leiper, Henry Smith. "It Depends on You." *Pacific Gas and Electric Progress* (245 Market St., San Francisco, Calif.).

CHAPTER II

PERSPECTIVE FOR THE SOCIAL STUDIES

According to legend, Daedalus and Icarus flew on wings of wax; Etana took flight on the back of an eagle; the King of Persia utilized a flying box propelled by eagles; and the Emperor of ancient Cathay traveled in airships to oversee his kingdom.

Nearly every student inquiring into the early development of air and space transportation takes delight from the mental images formulated by such tales. To the discerning teacher, such fascinating adventures serve a much broader purpose than the telling of a story or the disclosing of historical facts.

Children, caught up in the interesting tales but left to their own interpretations, may not discern the significance of the legends in relation to the emergence of air and space travel in the United States. The teacher, however, perceives that the information contained in the legends offers evidence from which pupils can discern that man in the earliest ages and in different parts of the world dreamed of flying. He realizes also that, as pupils acquire further information about the development of air and space travel, they can perceive that current achievements in the United States or any other nation are the outcome of hundreds of years of heroic sacrifice and experimentation. He is aware also that subsequent accumulation of many related pieces of information derived from investigating other aspects of cultural forms and processes leads pupils to generalize that no modern society has invented more than a fraction of its present culture. Thus, starting with pupils' ongoing and emerging interests in the evolution of air and space travel, the teacher helps pupils to move toward a major generalization from the field of anthropology.

An important role of the social studies is in orienting pupils as human beings, not only in space but in time.

Without a sense of indebtedness to what is around them in space and prior to them in time, children lose a sense of direction and the meaning of the values our society has selected to live by. Through the social studies, children can understand what man is and what he may become. The task of the teacher is to confront pupils with the contrasting worlds of different peoples and to cultivate skills of relating observations and descriptions of human affairs to personal interests, aspirations, and activities; to problems and other concerns of peers, friends, family, and society in general; and to significant concepts and generalizations, rules and principles, and laws and hypotheses about man in society.

Current emphasis with regard to the social studies is on reawakening the profession to the concept of the social studies as a dynamic area of the school curriculum, an area possessing substance and providing unique opportunities for helping children to understand the value systems of peoples and to develop the knowledge, attitudes, and skills needed in making important decisions affecting our society and our international relations.

The social studies has to be more than a reading period, more than a lecture by a person or team of persons. Man did not acquire his cultural heritage from secondary sources alone. He participated in the questioning, investigating, and the ordering of his world. One does not learn to play the piano by reading about, watching, or listening to people who play the piano; nor does one learn how to make decisions without making decisions; nor learn to organize materials without organizing them; nor learn to solve problems without solving them; nor learn to utilize knowledge without the opportunity to apply it in meaningful relationships. Replicating the discovery of knowledge is a prerequisite for acquiring the cultural heritage and is therefore a characteristic of the modern social studies.

Replicating the discovery of knowledge embodies not only commitment to developing and practicing the skills of inquiry, problem solving, and decision making but also use of primary sources of information. The basic source of information in modern social studies is to be found in the analysis of daily activities in one's own society.

The daily activities of each child and the affairs of the community provide a living laboratory for the study of cultural forms and processes. The concerns of mankind in places remote in time and space have a parallel in situations located in the here and now. Human concerns and problems encountered in protecting and conserving life and property; organizing and governing; communicating; educating; and creating tools and techniques, rituals and rites, and other universals of culture may be studied firsthand in parallel situations identified in a variety of home, school, and community settings. When a dispute over national boundaries can be perceived as similar to an issue of property rights between two people; the establishment of a common market, as similar to interstate commerce; the creation of a United Nations, as similar to other institutions designed to permit the peaceful solution of difficulties encountered, then pupils investigating the early development of Virginia, Kansas, Texas, or California or the mode of living in Africa, Latin America, or Japan are able to call forth understandings and attitudes that may enlighten comprehension of a situation far removed from their own in time, space, and complexity.

Activities such as interviewing, debating, observing, role playing adult experiences, and participating authentically in the fundamental work activities of people are not only important skills in themselves but are also important techniques in the structuring of the social studies as a laboratory subject. Such activities enable pupils to clarify thinking by placing themselves in significant situations, exercising control over the conditions, encountering the fundamental problems, delimiting solutions to the same basis of factors utilized by people in the culture studied, accepting the consequences of their actions, and reshaping the outcomes of the experiences in ways which make knowledge gained a tool to be utilized in further activities. In essence, these are the techniques of the social scientists who engage in on-the-spot inquiry into studies of societies and cultures.

Evidence exists to show that, unless the facts acquired from studies of cultures are organized around significant ideas, they are soon lost, become unwieldy, or remain useless. Opportunities must be planned for pupils to synthesize learnings, generalize information, and categorize knowledge in ways that are personal and unique. Many children will categorize information in similar ways; other children will select different methods of categorizing information. The divergent ordering of information often produces new and interesting perspectives from which to view subject matter while at the same time provides for developing and strengthening fundamental skills of inquiry and decision.

Included among the myriad of learnings children acquire are those that pertain to important ideas from the fields of anthropology, economics, geography, history, philosophy, political science, sociology, and social psychology. Since the information read about, observed, and listened to does not come neatly packaged into sets of facts and ideas related to specific generalizations, the teacher must take steps in planning instruction to identify the specific sets of facts contained in the books, films, study prints, maps, charts, and other instructional materials that offer evidence in support of a major generalization. First, the teacher must anticipate that pupils in the study of home and community will find out that on the street where they live—

1. Sand, rocks, cement, and water are mixed to make sidewalks, curbs, patios, and floors.

2. Sand, rocks, and oil are mixed together to make streets and playgrounds.

3. Vegetables and fruits grown in their backyards are gathered, processed, and eaten during their daily meals.

4. Certain houses are made from clay that has been converted into brick.

Then, knowing that the set of facts offers evidence that man in the local community converts the materials at hand to provide things he wants, the teacher is in a position to organize instruction so that pupils also can discern the relatedness of what appear to be isolated facts to a more central idea. The teacher can guide pupils to wonder if the first settlers in the local community also met their needs in a similar manner and whether people in distant places

and times also utilized materials of their geographic environment to satisfy fundamental needs and wants. In this manner, the generalization from geography derived from relatively meager information can become a hypothesis for further inquiry into cultural forms and processes. Then, when a study of a different society, culture, or region is undertaken by the class, pupils will be looking specifically to find out if people in a different setting also utilize geographic materials to satisfy their requirements. In essence, the pupils have participated in the task of evolving criteria for the study of cultures. The treatment of facts and other information derived in this manner from social studies activities makes possible the early development of important ideas that might otherwise be lost or delayed beyond the time of most effective learning.

An identification of basic understandings from the social sciences enables teachers to perceive organizing centers to which specific facts and other information from a variety of sources and topics throughout the grades may be related. In this view, concepts and generalizations are not taught per se but are outcomes from children's efforts to discern relatedness among the facts and information accumulated during social studies activities.

Major ideas from eight social science fields have been identified by social scientists working with the California State Department of Education during the years 1953 through 1961. The following synthesis of the basic ideas and concepts from each of the social sciences is useful to teachers for systemizing children's learnings.[1]

- Man's comprehension of the present and his wisdom in planning for the future depend upon his understanding of the events of the past that influence the present.

[1] *Building Curriculum in Social Studies for the Public Schools of California.* Bulletin of the California State Department of Education, May 1957. pp. 45-47. In synthesizing the major ideas from the eight social sciences, recognition is given to the possibility of error of interpretation in attempting to reduce the number of concepts and to restate the basic ideas. Thus, the wisdom of referring to the separate lists from each of the social sciences for purposes of curriculum planning is advocated.

- Change is a condition of human society; civilizations rise and fall; value systems improve or deteriorate; the tempo of change varies with cultures and periods of history.

- Through all time and in all regions of the world, man has worked to meet common basic human needs and to satisfy common human desires and aspirations.

- People of all races, religions, and cultures have contributed to the cultural heritage. Modern society owes a debt to cultural inventors of other places and times.

- Interdependence is a constant factor in human relationships. The realization of self develops through contact with others. Social groupings of all kinds develop as a means of group cooperation in meeting individual and societal needs.

- The culture under which an individual is reared and the social groups to which he belongs exert great influence on his ways of perceiving, thinking, feeling, and acting.

- Democracy is dependent on the process of free inquiry; this process provides for defining the problem, seeking data, using the scientific method in collecting evidence, restating the problem in terms of its interrelationships, arriving at a principle that is applicable, and applying the principle in the solution of the problem.

- The basic substance of a civilization is rooted in its values, and the nature of the values is the most persistent and important problem faced by human beings.

- Man must make choices based on economic knowledge, scientific comparisons, analytic judgment, and his value system concerning how he will use the resources of the world.

- The work of society is done through organized groups; and group membership involves opportunities, responsibilities, and the development of leadership.

- Organized group life of all types must act in accordance with established rules of social relationships and a system of social controls.

- All nations of the modern world are part of a global, independent system of economic, social, cultural, and political life.

- Democracy is based on belief in equality of opportunity, man's integrity, the individual's dignity, man's rationality, man's goodness, man's practicality, and man's ability to govern himself and solve his problems cooperatively.

- Anthropologists hold that, physically, man is the product of the same biological evolution as the rest of the animal kingdom. Man is similar to other animals in many ways, but a most important difference exists in man's rationality and in the body of knowledge, beliefs, and values which constitutes man's culture.

- All human beings are of one biological species within which occur variations, or races. The differences between races are negligible.

- Environment affects man's way of living, and man in turn modifies his environment.

- One of the factors affecting man's mode of life is his natural environment. Weather and climate that cause regional differences in land forms, soils, drainage, and natural vegetation determine the relative density of population in the various regions of the world.

- Because man must use natural resources to survive, the distribution and use of these resources determine where he lives on the earth's surface and to some extent how well he lives. The level of his technology determines how he produces, exchanges, transports, and consumes his goods.

The teacher, faced with the task of helping pupils to acquire important adult generalizations, must deductively break down the big idea into its component parts.

The generalization—*man utilizes the materials of his geographic environment to fulfill fundamental wants*—involves concepts about (a) man, (b) utilization, (c) materials, (d) geographic environment, (e) fulfillment, and (f) fundamental wants. Knowledge about each of these concepts is joined to produce the generalization from cultural geography.

Information accumulated throughout the ages, describing how man in differing ages, social roles, and ethnic situations in contrasting time and space patterns utilized materials from his geographic environment to fulfill wants, is embodied in the concept of *man*.

Information describing techniques through which differing, definitive categories of man gather and process materials as in cutting, shaping, cleaning, cooking, welding, and pounding to extend their utility is embodied in the concept of *utilization*. Likewise, all known vegetable, mineral, gaseous, and synthetic substances are included in the concept of *materials*. Similar consideration is given to the variety of forms of satisfaction connoting the term, *fulfillment;* whereas the concept of *fundamental wants* includes food, clothing, shelter, transportation, communication, education, government, record keeping, and other universals of culture.

Having identified the major concepts which make up the generalization from cultural geography, the task is to identify the examples of human activities observable in the classroom, home, and community and in the content of textbooks, films, and other instructional materials that show the ways in which man uses the materials of his geographic environment to satisfy wants and needs.

Relating the learning activities planned to help children at every grade level in their inquiry into cultural forms and processes to the big ideas from the social sciences is a major task for each teacher. To do this, the teacher must perceive the relatedness of the pupils' experiences to the facts and other information accruing from the activities and must identify the relatedness of the facts to the development of major concepts and generalizations.

The teacher, knowing that pupils in a study of home and community acquire evidence that man converts the materials of his local geographical environment to satisfy needs, recognizes that the study of Mexico or Japan or Africa offers pupils opportunity to apply the hypothesis formulated earlier to a new situation. Thus, a purpose for planning certain activities for a study of Mexico is, in this case, to help children to realize that man in Mexico uses the materials of his geographic environment to fulfill his needs.

The purpose of pupils is likely to be personal and specific in contrast to the broader societal and intellectual purpose held by the teacher. In planning an activity, the teacher might identify his purpose and that of the pupils as follows:

Teacher Purpose	Pupils Purpose
To help pupils to realize that man uses the materials in his geographic environment to fulfill needs and desires for shelter.	To find out the type of shelter they would live in if they were Mexican citizens living in Taxco, Tepozatlan, or another village in which the study was centered.

From discussing ideas gleaned through reading, study trips, interviews, study prints, films, and filmstrips, pupils acquire many facts about many topics other than shelter. The subsequent experience of reshaping the information through classifying, organizing, and recording facts and ideas on charts, graphs, pictorial maps, murals, and other graphic forms enables pupils to identify related facts about shelter and other cultural categories. The relatedness of specific facts about shelter to the activities provided may be anticipated by the teacher as follows:

Experiences Involved	Data Discovered
Raising the question: What types of shelter are used in Taxco, Tepozatlan, or another locality in which the study is centered?	People in certain areas of Mexico build houses completely of thatch gathered in the local area.
Hypothesizing about the kind of shelter appropriate to the village.	People in certain parts of Mexico build houses of lumber cut in nearby forests.
Examining study prints, photographs, slides, and magazine illustrations of homes in Mexico.	People in many parts of Mexico convert the adobe soil from their land into bricks to construct shelters.

Experiences Involved (con't.)

Examining shelters in the local area that help to clarify thinking about the types of shelters identified.

Looking at films and television broadcasts that portray the shelters pertinent to the area of study.

Reading from all available sources about the kinds of shelters used in the region of Tepozatlan, Taxco, or other areas of Mexico.

Questioning the authenticity of the information gathered and its appropriateness in obtaining a reliable solution to the problem.

Verifying or disqualifying the original statements made regarding their beliefs about the type of shelter to be found in a particular area of Mexico.

Data Discovered (con't.)

People in certain areas of Mexico construct houses of scrap materials such as wooden boxes, tin containers, and pieces of heavy cardboard gathered from the dump heaps of the countryside.

People in certain parts of Mexico gather large stones from the countryside to erect shelters.

Data Discovered (con't.)

People in certain parts of Mexico build houses of lumber cut in nearby forests.

People in many parts of Mexico convert the adobe soil from their land into bricks to construct shelters.

People in certain areas of Mexico construct houses of scrap materials gathered from local dump heaps.

People in certain parts of Mexico gather large stones from the land to erect shelters.

Subsequent experiences of gathering information and synthesizing and generalizing the data enable pupils to evolve similar concepts and subgeneralizations. The accumulation of related concepts is shown in the following manner:

Concepts Derived	Subgeneralizations Evolved
People in Mexico use materials in the local environment to fulfill needs and wants for shelter.	Man uses materials in his geographic environment to fulfill needs and wants for shelter.
People in Mexico use materials in the local environment to fulfill needs and wants for clothing.	Man uses materials in his geographic environment to fulfill needs and wants for clothing.
People in Mexico use materials in the local environment to fulfill needs and wants for food.	Man uses materials in his geographic environment to fulfill needs and wants for food.

Guided activities of synthesizing and generalizing the facts and ideas obtained from inquiry enable pupils to arrive at the same or similar concept about shelter as that held by the teacher. The relatedness of the facts to a concept about shelter is identified as follows:

Data Discovered	Concept Derived
People in certain areas of Mexico build houses completely of thatch gathered in the local area.	People in Mexico use materials at hand in the local environment to satisfy need for shelter.

Similar investigation of the mode of living of people in contrasting time and place settings enables pupils to evolve the adult-held generalization that man utilizes the materials of his environment to fulfill fundamental needs and wants.

Relatedness among each of the various elements in the teaching-learning activity from its genesis in the purposes of teacher and pupils to the evolution of major concepts and generalizations from cultural geography may be discerned more clearly by examining the constructs on page 18.

The same generalization can be developed over a period of several years as pupils study contrasting patterns of cultures provided that the sets of related facts are brought forward from study to study and reconsidered in the light of new information. In this manner, concepts and generalizations may be re-enforced, modified, or discarded.

The chart on page 19 reveals how a concept and generalization may be developed throughout the grades.

The social studies, through a study of contrasting patterns of cultures possessing divergent value systems, geographical variables, and alternative solutions to fundamental problems, offer unique opportunities for pupils to study and to practice techniques for inquiry, problem solving, and decision making. From the stress on the inductive processes for learning in which instruction centers on the active involvement of children in making decisions, solving problems, gathering, synthesizing, and classifying data, inference is made that primary sources of information need increased attention and utilization.

The social studies embody a search for truth. A multidisciplinary approach is needed to assure pupils the power and the ability to understand the great variations in human ingenuity and achievements. In the words of Jerome Bruner, what is emerging in the social studies today as a mark of our generation "is a widespread renewal of concern for the quality and intellectual aims of education . . . but without abandonment of the ideal that education should serve as a means of training well-balanced citizens for a democracy." [2]

[2] Bruner, Jerome S. *The Process of Education.* Cambridge, Mass.: Harvard University Press, 1961. p. 1.

The role of a citizen involves certain behaviors. The focus today is on building the meanings and the skills of citizenship to such an extent that they become part of the make-up of each person, invoking automatic response to appropriate stimuli, i.e., becoming a habit. Thus, when one is faced with making a decision, as in voting, one automatically strives to become thoroughly informed on the issues, studying each issue from a variety of points of view and making a wise choice for himself. Both the act of voting and the penetrating study of the issues would be natural responses by each person. In order to bring about this outcome, the social studies program needs to be viewed as a dynamic aspect of every school curriculum, a time for trying out the behaviors already learned, for testing ideas procured from the studies of contrasting patterns of cultures, for perceiving the relatedness of school and subject matter to establishing and maintaining values subscribed to, and for practicing the behaviors that are necessary to a retention of basic values. We need to reverse the conventional pattern for learning. We ask pupils to learn answers to things for which they do not even perceive questions. We need to seek ways of helping children raise increasingly significant questions, devise their own solutions, identify and explore alternative solutions, and evaluate their achievement in terms of significant criteria which they have helped to develop. The social studies can provide the setting in which pupils can participate actively in the investigation of contrasting systems of cultural forms and processes. The inquiry into contrasting patterns of cultures by pupils enables them to evolve, try out, and practice skills of perceiving significant relationships, questioning, hypothesizing, gathering information, classifying and synthesizing raw data, and making decisions in light of conflicting information. These outcomes depend on the insights which curriculum makers and teachers can bring to the social studies as a dynamic area of the curriculum possessing unique opportunities for the development of social and intellectual powers.

Teacher Purpose	Pupils Purpose
To help children to realize that man uses the materials of his geographic environment to fulfill needs and desires for shelter.	To find out the type of shelter the class would live in if they were Mexican settlers in Tepozatlan, Taxco, or another village in which the study centered.

Experiences Involved

Raising the question: What types of shelter are used in Taxco, Tepozatlan, or another locality in which the study is centered?

Hypothesizing about the kind of shelter appropriate to the village.

Examining study prints, photographs, photographs, slides, and magazine illustrations of homes in Mexico.

Examining firsthand those shelters in the local area that help to clarify thinking about the types of shelters identified.

Looking at films and television broadcasts that portray the shelters pertinent to the area of study.

Reading from all available sources about the kinds of shelters utilized in the region of Tepozatlan and other areas of Mexico.

Questioning the authenticity of the information gathered and its appropriateness in obtaining a reliable solution to the problem.

Verifying or disqualifying the original statements made regarding the type of shelter they would live in.

Data Discovered

People in certain areas of Mexico build houses completely of thatch gathered in the local area.

People in certain parts of Mexico build houses of lumber.

People in certain parts of Mexico convert the adobe soil from their land into bricks to construct their homes.

People in certain areas of Mexico construct houses of scrap materials such as wooden boxes, large tin containers, and pieces of heavy cardboard gathered from the dump heaps of the countryside.

People in certain parts of Mexico gather large stones from the surrounding countryside to erect shelters.

Concept Derived

People in Mexico use materials at hand to construct their shelters.

Subgeneralization Evolved

Man utilizes the abundant materials at hand to fulfill his wants and needs for shelter.

Generalization Emerging

Subsequent Teacher Purposes

Man in Mexico uses the materials in his geographic environment to fulfill needs and desires for clothing.

Man in Mexico uses the materials in his geographic environment to fulfill needs and desires for food.

Subsequent Pupils Purposes

To find out the types of clothing the class would wear if they lived in Tepozatlan, Taxco, or another village.

To find out the kinds of foods they would eat if they were Mexican people living in Tepozatlan, Taxco, or another village.

Subsequent Concepts

People in Mexico use materials at hand to make their clothing.

People in Mexico use the items in the local area to satisfy requirements for food.

Subsequent Subgeneralizations

Man utilizes the abundant materials at hand to fulfill his wants and needs for clothing.

Man utilizes the abundant materials at hand to fulfill his wants and needs for food.

Subsequent experiences involved produce new facts and other information that lead in turn to new understandings.

The accumulation of subgeneralizations moves pupils toward the basic generalization that

Man utilizes the abundant materials in his geographic environment to fulfill fundamental wants and needs.[3]

---

[3] This generalization is a subgeneralization of the broader idea identified in the synthesis of generalizations presented earlier in this chapter which states that, through all time and in all regions of the world, man has worked to meet common basic needs and to satisfy common human desires and aspirations.

Teacher Purpose

To help children to realize that man uses the materials of his geographic environment to fulfill needs and desires for shelter.

Pupils Purpose

To find out the type of shelter they would live in if they were to be settlers in the particular region being investigated.

Experiences Involved

Raising the question: What types of shelter are used in Taxco, Tepoztlan, or another locality in which the study is centered?

Hypothesizing about the kind of shelter appropriate to the era and region under study.

Examining study prints, photographs, filmstrips, and magazine pictures showing shelters appropriate to the region being studied.

Examining shelters in the local area that clarify thinking about the types of shelters identifed during the study.

Looking at films and television broadcasts that portray shelters pertinent to the area of study.

Reading from all available sources about the kinds of shelters utilized by the society being investigated.

Questioning the authenticity of the information gathered and its appropriateness in obtaining a reliable solution to the problem.

Verifying or disqualifying the original statements made regarding beliefs about the types of shelter available in the culture under study.

Data Discovered

People in the local community mix sand, rocks, and cement to construct shelters.

People in the early days of Los Angeles convert adobe soil into bricks to construct shelters.

People in the gold fields build shelters of large rocks gathered from the area.

People in Tepoztlan make adobe brick to provide shelters.

People in Ghana make shelters from poles and grasses cut from the nearby area.

Pilgrims convert logs from nearby forests into planks and shakes to construct shelters.

Settlers in the prairie regions of North America live in sod houses.

Plains Indians live in shelters made from the skins of animals they killed.

Eskimo houses are made from large blocks of ice and are called igloos.

Concepts Derived

People in California use materials at hand to construct shelters.

People in Mexico use materials at hand to construct shelters.

People in the colonies use materials at hand to construct shelters.

People in the prairie regions use materials at hand to construct shelters.

People in the plains regions during time of abundant game use the materials at hand for constructing shelters.

People in Alaska use abundant materials at hand for constructing shelters.

Subgeneralization Evolved

Man utilizes the abundant materials at hand to fulfill his wants and needs for shelter.

Generalization Emerging

Similar experiences of pupils in gathering information about clothing and food lead to the evolution of concepts about clothing and food.

Subsequent Concepts

People in California, Mexico, and the colonies use the materials at hand to fulfill wants and needs for clothing.

People in California, Mexico, and the colonies use materials at hand to fulfill wants and needs for food.

Subsequent Subgeneralizations

Man utilizes the abundant materials at hand to fulfill his wants and needs for clothing.

Man utilizes the abundant materials at hand to fulfill his wants and needs for food.

Man utilizes the abundant materials in his geographic environment to satisfy fundamental wants and needs.

CHAPTER III

GUIDING CHILDREN THROUGH THE

SOCIAL STUDIES

IN THE PRIMARY GRADES

Modern education reflects a concern for the characteristics of children, as they are, as they grow, and what they become as a result of the guidance through the educative processes. This chapter gives attention to the teaching of the social studies in accordance with knowledge about child growth and development, the subject matter to be learned, and the processes through which children come into possession of the subject matters of the school.

The Children Are. Imagination and curiosity spark the young child. Although he is inquisitive about his immediate environment, he is constantly pushing against the boundaries of time and space as he explores his world. The veneer of society may be readily apparent to the child. However, what lies beneath the veneer may be noticed only superficially. The child usually sees much more than he tells, yet implications and insights as to the "why" of a situation may still be relatively unknown.

The world of the child is expanding. Through modern transportation facilities, the neighborhood is becoming much more than a small geographic slice of home and the immediate area surrounding it. Many children have not only traveled extensively in the United States but abroad as well. Through the medium of television, the world of fact and fiction is brought directly into the home in a highly impressive manner. The vivid imagery of television transplants the child's home into the environments of all parts of the world. For many children, particularly those in suburban and urban areas, the local environment may be less familiar than those places which are a considerable distance from home.

The years of early childhood are of great importance because they include the time when children first begin to develop understandings about man's ways of living in the world and universe. The more extensive the concepts, knowledges, and skills developed in the social studies, the stronger will be the foundation on which young children may move ahead to deepen their understanding of human interrelationships, man to man, and man to environment.

Research has demonstrated that young children have an amazing capacity for learning. Parents and teachers observe rapid changes as children acquire skills, information, and values. Through sensory experience and muscular activities, the inquisitive mind of the young child generates questions. These create a need for communication and provide spurs to creative expression.

How do these children become one with their environment? How can each child gain the personal skills which are necessary in a society in which every person is expected to work individually as well as cooperatively with others? How can the experiences the school provides equip children to assume the privileges and obligations of citizenship in a democracy?

The Children Grow. Many varied experiences are necessary for young children because each child differs in experiential background, interests, temperament, sensory perception, and intelligence. Through the social studies, instruction can be planned in terms of the variety of needs of each child, so that it is possible to provide for growth in many ways. Experiences are provided which enable children to challenge and to speculate about the kinds of changes taking place within their environment.

Change is inevitable in our society. The mature citizen needs to understand change and to make reasonable and significant decisions concerning it. Activities should be provided for young children which will help them to relate information about any generalization such as change. Children should be given opportunities to develop ideas; these ideas should be checked in a variety of ways to see if they are understood. By providing experiences that call for application as well as for verbalization, the learner's understanding of the idea is checked.

A group of kindergarten children watched with consternation as heavy machines moved onto the grassy open lot near the school. The children remembered the fun of running up the little hill with the wind in their faces. From the very top under the sheltering oak tree, they had surveyed the world, sailed to faraway lands on imaginary voyages, and relived a dozen other adventures. Now all this was to be changed. The grass was plowed under; men and machines began to level the little hill.

The questions the children asked were accepted with respect and interest by the teacher and the foreman on the job. The children's ideas were considered of value. In return, the youngsters listened to the reasons why the use of the land was being changed. They began to grow in understanding that land may be used for many purposes. They realized that another shopping center was increasingly important as more and more families moved into the new homes nearby.

Older primary children continue to grow in critical thinking and questioning as they observe the many subdivisions replacing acres of fruit orchards and farm lands or as they study the building of highways that cut across land previously used for agricultural or other purposes. In the process, children ask questions such as these:

Why do we need so many highways?

What will people do for fruit and vegetables when farm land is covered with houses and highways?

Why do people have to sell their good farm land?

What happens if people want to keep their land?

Where do all the new people in our community come from?

Why do people come to our community?

Freedom to question, to be informed about and to act upon the need for change is a responsibility of citizenship. Understanding and knowledge of the past enables the child to realize that change is a condition of human society in the present and may be expected in the future. Social studies experiences provide significant opportunities for encouraging children to look at various elements of a situation, to be selective in choosing the important ones, and to seek multiple answers to problems.

If change is normal and to be expected, critical thinking and evaluation skills must be acquired and strengthened.

Emphasis needs to be directed to the "why" and "how" of information as much as to the "what" and "who." Boys and girls need to see that there may be multiple answers to problems; that there may be more than one right answer; that there may be many ways to seek answers; and that people tend to relate the correctness of any answer to themselves and their personal needs.

In order to understand relationships, children need to see life in more than one dimension. In the study of the home, it is essential that children see that, in all cultures, fathers and mothers do not have identical roles. Whereas the father may be the basic worker in the American home, in other parts of the world the mother may do the heavy work. Even in the United States, patterns are shifting so that many women share the wage-earning responsibilities of a household. In some parts of the world, marriage does not mean breaking up a household; instead, the son and his wife move into the same general compound extending the size and capabilities of the home and family. The requirements of a boy or girl in Indian households may not be the same as those of children in American homes. Children and teachers need to become much more familiar with the various patterns of social structure within the United States as well as the multiple patterns of living practiced throughout the world. In the study of any aspect of community life, it is possible to look at more than just the local area. Comparisons and contrasts are possible with many parts of the world.

Through the study of Indian and other cultures less industrialized and complex than their own, children find that people often solve quite similar problems in diverse ways. Geographical and historical ideas become important to children as they seek to explain cultural similarities and differences. Approaching the study from an anthropological point of view helps children to uncover stereotypes and replace them with accurate information and more precise understandings.

A group of primary children, studying the Hopis, were asked what an Indian really was. The original concept of the children was that an Indian was a person who wore few clothes, had a feathered headdress, rode a horse, scalped whites, and whose entire conversation consisted of either wild whoops or monosyllabic grunts. The teacher asked questions such as the following: If I wore a headdress, would I be an Indian? Are all horseback riders Indians? If I grunt or make a whoop, does that make me an Indian? If an Indian makes his clothes look like the clothing other people wear, would he still be an Indian?

The children quickly realized that their criteria would not distinguish Indians from other groups, particularly Indians living today. An interview with an Indian living in the community and working as an engineer in a local factory helped to dispel some of the misconceptions. In the course of many discussions and considerable research, terms such as *Negro, Caucasian, Mongoloid,* and *native* became familiar to the children. The children learned some of the theories as to how Indians first came to America. The jigsaw possibilities in the theory of the floating continents fascinated the children. Most of them were unaware of why these people were given the name, *Indian*. Particularly interesting to the group was the realization that each child was a native of some area, a contrast from their original belief that a native was a member of some primitive tribal group who went around in his environment virtually naked.

At the end of the study, children were able to distinguish between Indians of the pre-Columbus period, Indians involved in the western migration of people from the United States, Indians of North and South America, and Indians of today. The basic physiological characteristics distinguishing Indians from other racial groups were noted. From this series of activities, the children realized that all mankind is essentially more alike than different in terms of physical characteristics and needs.

When the children were again asked, "What is an Indian?" they were no longer satisfied with answers gained from television or motion pictures. They were able to approach a definition based on anthropological and sociological criteria and expressed a greater depth of understanding of the Indians both as a group of people and as individuals.

Observing and learning about the interdependence of people and nations are vital parts of the social studies program.

Young children become aware that individual members of a family have different and special roles long before they enter school. In kindergarten, they develop an appreciation of differences in homes; they learn that people are dependent upon each other. By the end of the first year in school, most children have acquired understandings which enable them to make generalizations such as the following:

1. Individual members of a family are interdependent.
2. Cooperation permits many areas of specialized work.
3. Families are dependent upon many people.
4. Communication and transportation foster interdependence.

Children, throughout the grades, continue to develop such generalizations as the following about the community:

1. People work together to modify the environment in order to meet many of their needs.
2. Rural and urban communities are increasingly interdependent.
3. Nations and communities are dependent upon one another for the raw materials and manufactured goods they need or desire.

Through careful planning for experiential and developmental activities, such generalizations become part of a primary child's understanding. This goal is not accomplished by the mere acquisition of facts and information. The value and use of what is taught depends upon how it is taught. The educator's role is to arrange a stimulating and significant environment to enable children to take part in decision making in their daily experiences. Through the evaluation of these decisions, children are helped to accept, modify, or change their actions in order to achieve desired social goals. Of equal importance, they are made aware of the decision-making process itself.

The process of decision making by a group usually involves—

1. The identification of the problem.
2. The identification of pertinent questions to ask.
3. The withdrawal of personal feelings by each individual in the group in order to focus better on the problem.
4. The formulation of several hypotheses.
5. The exploration of ideas and words involved in the hypotheses.
6. The identification of reliable sources of data.
7. Research and experimentation to test each of the hypotheses.
8. The utilization of reliable sources of data.
9. Selection of tentative solution(s).
10. Action based upon tentative solution(s).
11. Evaluation of success or failure of action.
12. Acceptance, modification, or rejection of solution(s).

In this process of inquiry, the teacher and children continually use all available resources—textbooks, trade books, films, encyclopedias, magazines, resource people, study trips, experiments, observations, demonstrations, and interviews. Children construct and make things in order to understand the processes by which man changes raw materials into finished products. Aesthetic experiences are gained through music, art, and literature. Children share and report through discussions, writing stories, poems, and songs, painting pictures or murals, map making, dramatic representation, and expressions through bodily movement. Through group cooperation and planning, skills in doing research, reporting, comparing, relating, summarizing, and generalizing are developed.

As an example of the above processes in community studies usually pursued in the primary school curriculum, it is important for children to gain understandings which will lead to making generalizations about interdependence. As children become concerned about the distribution of food in an area, they learn of the need for interdependence. Through discussion and dramatization, the children find out what the group already knows and what additional knowledge is needed. Then they talk to truck drivers, farmers, and grocery clerks and take a trip to the wholesale market to study the operations of the marketing system and to talk with the workers. Such activities allow them to consolidate their learnings and to relate the learnings to generalizations about the interdependence of the people. Understandings in the fields of economics and political science soon evolve.

The same process may be followed when children are studying another culture. The teacher provides activities designed to build upon the concepts acquired in previous studies. Erroneous ideas are clarified through research, discussion, dramatization, construction, the graphic arts, and problem solving. Experiences at the child's level enable learnings to take place, directions for investigation to be set, and new purposes for learning to be identified.

As children study a culture, their questions guided by the teacher revolve not only around what is alike or different but why it is alike or different. The customs and the artifacts of another cultural group help children appreciate what they know of interdependence not only in their country but in other lands as well. Children come gradually to realize that people of all races, religions, and cultures have contributed to our heritage. Not only are we interrelated by our very humanness but also by present world needs which nurture interdependence more and more.

Seeking solutions to the persistent problems which perplex mankind draws upon the knowledge and skills refined and organized into the various social science fields. While we have generally accepted such categories as anthropology, economics, geography, history, philosophy, political science, social psychology, and sociology as discrete social sciences, all of the separate social sciences are so inextricably interwoven in the affairs of mankind that they defy separation by teacher, pupil, and social scientist alike. One of the major tasks confronting the teacher of the social studies today is to provide activities designed to help children to discover both the interrelationships among the social sciences and the everyday affairs of their society. The chart on page 25 reveals certain of the interrelationships inherent within a study of homes in the community.

Similar analyses could be made of other aspects of any community structure. Only when the teacher perceives the relatedness of the studies to subject matter fields and to important ideas within any area can he knowingly help children to identify such relatedness.

The Children Become. In the year 2000, children who are currently in the primary school will be in the prime of their adult years. What happens in the schools of today will be a vital ingredient in determining the success of the future. A look at the past should be sufficient to indicate that change will be an essential ingredient of society in this and every succeeding year. No longer can any school hope to teach all of the knowledge known to the world. Even if this were possible, within ten years much of this knowledge would be outdated, discarded, or disproved. It is increasingly important, therefore, that children learn that school is not a terminal point of education but a springboard into the challenging frontiers of future years. Children need to learn various ways of acquiring information upon which to base action in a world which is constantly changing.

From a broad base of experience, the social studies provide ample opportunities for children to acquire meanings and skills upon which to base action. However, experience by itself is no guarantee that learning will take place as desired. Children have thousands of distinct experiences daily; they are probably unaware of most of them. Often, experience is derived basically from the written word in a book or the spoken word of the teacher. It is the task of the teacher to help children to see the variegated colors of the grasses in the field, the many sounds of life hidden within the terrain about them, the bird's nest concealed in the tree, the rutted road which guides them safely to a given destination, as well as the variety of meanings which serve the words contained on the printed page. Through dramatic play, rhythmic activities, art, music, and creative writing, children can organize what they know and feel. Only then do they become a basic part of one's being.

Each child relates what is to be learned to his experience, the environment in which he finds himself, and the moment in time of the lesson itself. How the child perceives the

SOCIOLOGY

Why do we live in homes?
What does the mother do in the home?
What does the father do in the home?
What do children do in the home?
What do mothers, fathers, and children do when they are not at home?
Who is a member of the family?
Where did the family come from?
Why do parents have to work?
Why do children have to go to school?

HISTORY

What were homes like which were built by early man?
Why did early man build homes in so many different ways?
What were the first homes like where we now live?
What was my family's first home like?
Who built the first homes in our area?

ANTHROPOLOGY

Why did the first people come to our area to live?
Do all children leave their homes when they get married?
What kinds of homes do people have in other parts of the world?
Are there different ways of getting food, clothing, shelter, and utensils for homes?
Are there different kinds of food, clothing, shelter, and utensils in homes throughout the world?
What kinds of jobs do our parents have and where do they work?

POLITICAL SCIENCE

Can we build a house in any place we want?
Can we do anything that we want to in our house?
Who protects our house?

A STUDY OF HOMES
First Grade

PSYCHOLOGY

Why is it important that all people work together?
When do people work for themselves and when do they work for others?
What's the best way to solve problems?

GEOGRAPHY

What is the shape of my house?
What are the shapes of the rooms in my house?
Where is my house located in the community?
Why do people build houses?
Where do people get the materials to build houses?
What materials are used to build houses?
Why doesn't everyone live in the same kind of house?
Why do so many people usually decide to live together in the same area?
Why do some houses have flat roofs and some houses have roofs which slant?

PHILOSOPHY

Why do we need to solve problems?
Is there sometimes more than one right answer?
Is there sometimes more than one way to get an answer?
Should things always be the same?

ECONOMICS

Who builds houses?
How many kinds of jobs are needed in order to build a house?
Who pays the men who work on the jobs?
Why do they use machines?
Why do some builders like to build many houses in the same area and at the same time?
Why are so many different kinds of houses needed?
How do the builders know where to put everything?
Do all people own their houses?
Who helps people to buy houses if they don't have enough money?

lesson is perhaps as important as the teacher's conception of what is being said or demonstrated. The teacher's ear must be tuned to the unspoken question often hidden in the context of the child's spoken word. Children's unusual responses need to be valued, considered, and examined. Children should be encouraged to ask questions, develop methods for answering their questions, and evaluate the authenticity of each of their responses; they should be constantly challenged to look beyond the superficial, the obvious, and the easiest.

Children begin to solve problems soon after birth. By the time they enter school, inquiry capabilities are quite well developed. Through discussion, reading, dramatic play, rhythm, music, art, out-of-school experiences, and study trips, many important problems calling for knowledge and skills in the social sciences occur. Part of the skill of teaching is arranging situations to make sure that problems *will* occur. The skillful teacher encourages the identification of a wide range of hypotheses making before permitting children to try to solve the problem. Rather than indicating the correct answer or answers and short-cutting the learning act, the teacher permits all answers to be considered and evaluated by the children. Children learn that their opinions are valued but that they need to be evaluated. One significant lesson learned from the inductive processes for solving difficulties is that selecting the correct question may be much more important in solving a problem than looking initially for the correct answer.

What will the children become? First, they will be human beings who are willing to think about ideas derived from relevant data rather than to become repositories of unrelated facts which are quickly and often conveniently forgotten. Secondly, they will be learners with a growing ability to relate fact and experience, weaving these into a framework of relationships. Thirdly, they will begin to develop skills, attitudes, appreciations, and understandings which will enable them to become more effective learners in the upper grades and eventually to develop the qualities that characterize a participating, thinking, mature citizen.

CHAPTER IV

GUIDING CHILDREN THROUGH THE
SOCIAL STUDIES
IN THE INTERMEDIATE GRADES

Children entering the intermediate grades are in possession of a wide assortment of information about the affairs of mankind, accumulated through their out-of-school observations and their in-school studies during the primary years. During the intermediate years, children will continue to engage in the quest for information about ways in which man strives to gain increasing control over his daily activities. The task of sorting out the significant facts and ideas worthy of acquisition and retention is a complex matter. Children require guidance in devising and practicing ways of sorting data, organizing information for further use and longer retention, and reshaping knowledge into useful forms.

It is in the processes of sorting, organizing, and reshaping knowledge that children acquire insights into the relatedness of the school curriculum to problems of personal as well as broader societal significance. If the social studies period is to have meaning and not become a school subject of dubious value, it seems imperative that children be helped to discern relatedness of their learning activities and experiences to (a) personal interests, aspirations, and activities; (b) problems and other concerns of peers, friends, family, and society in general; (c) other in-school studies; and (d) significant concepts and generalizations, rules and principles, and laws and hypotheses about man in society.

Fundamental to the task of establishing relationships is the teacher's recognition of (a) significant concepts and generalizations from the social sciences and related natural sciences; (b) analogies, examples, or "for instances" which may be drawn from children's daily activities and from the recorded accounts of man's activities throughout the ages substantiating the rules, principles, laws, generalizations, and hypotheses governing man; and (c) ways of reshaping information so that the examples, analogies, and "for instances" stand forth for each child as insights growing out of the child's pursuit of broader inquiry into the activities of mankind.

Utilizing the local community as a living laboratory for the study of cultures is a concept subscribed to by many teachers of modern day social studies. The assumption that a person is better able to understand his community through comparative studies of communities that contrast greatly with it is also accepted by teachers of modern social studies programs. Viewing the community as a living laboratory together with the selection of contrasting patterns of cultures as vehicles for study underlies the current practice of selecting a particular culture and studying it in depth during each semester of the intermediate grades. An important implication for the teacher is that he not only must acquire a strong background of knowledge regarding the important ideas from the social sciences, the techniques utilized by social scientists in conducting inquiry, and a thorough knowledge of the culture that is to serve as the structure of interest and investigation but also must perceive relatedness among the interests of people remote in time and space to children's interests here and now; of problems and concerns of people in different regions of the globe to issues and concerns in the home and local communities; of means-to-end patterns of other cultures to means-to-end relationships at home, at school, and in the community, state, and nation.

An arranged environment for a study of culture is an asset for a laboratory approach to that study. If the culture is a local one, then the observation and analysis of the daily activities of the people at home, in the neighborhood, community, state, or nation become the bases for inquiry and of sources of knowledge. The concept of the classroom is broadened to encompass the daily activities of mankind away from the school. On-the-spot study of human affairs constitutes a major aspect of the social studies program. In such a structure, it is not too difficult to help children note that an issue of property rights in Cuba or Berlin has relatedness to the issue of colonization in Africa, the dispute over water rights between California and Arizona, or possession of the fire truck in the kindergarten sandbox.

In an effort to help children perceive the study of cultures as a source for understanding not only the activities, aspirations, and motivations of people in other lands but also their own state and nation as well, one creative teacher organized a cultural laboratory for the study of Japan.[1] Inasmuch as the children could not visit Japan for firsthand study in the manner of the social scientists, an arranged environment was created to make possible strong personal identification by children with the Japanese people. The basic assumption was that, when children can put themselves in the place of the Japanese people through replicating certain fundamental activities of the people in a realistic setting, children find themselves inside the culture. In the process of matching ideas and feelings with the Japanese parent, laborer, merchant, religious leader, or other agent in society, children encounter the basic problems, devise similar or identical solutions to difficulties, and acquire insight into the aspirations, values, and activities of the people living in Japan and the mutual concerns regarding the mode of living in their community, state, or nation. The arranged environment and the replication of fundamental processes of Japanese society in authentic ways through experiences of dramatic representation, industrial arts, song, dance, art, and language provide children with an opportunity to take on the identity of a Japanese father, mother, rice grower, textile worker, school teacher, merchant, politician, or religious leader to see what it is like to be on the inside of an important social situation and to exercise control over the conditions. A description of the arranged environment created for a study of Japan follows.

ENVIRONMENT

Authentic Japanese household items were arranged in one corner of the room. Two sliding panels provided the walls for the home. Straw *tatami* matting covered one section of the floor. A small, low table was in the center of the room. The rice container with its flat wooden server was in the

---

[1] The pattern which follows is applicable to a study of any social unit, society, or culture at the local, state, regional, national, or world level.

center of the table. Rope sandals were on the floor in one corner. The *geta* ("clogs") were by the entry. On a low table in another corner was a quilt and *happi* coat. A set of ceremonial tea utensils was ready to be used. A kettle was waiting to be filled with water. The *kakemoni* ("hanging scroll") hung from the wall. There was a *Shinto kamidana* ("God-shelf") and a miniature Buddhist temple.

A variety of miniature plants from a Japanese garden were on a table and outside the wall of the house. A picture of a Japanese garden with the Shinto gate hung on the wall above the table. A variety of books on many levels of difficulty, opened to reveal various aspects of Japanese life, were displayed on a table.

Another table displayed a variety of Japanese foods such as rice, dried seaweed, dried squid, tuna, tea leaves, and *kasutera* ("sponge cake"). Above the table were pictures of Japanese fishermen unloading their catch of fish, men and women transplanting rice, men making charcoal, and Japanese women shopping in a western-style market.

On another table there was an arrangement of a kimono, *zori,* and *geta.* Books were opened to illustrations of women working in a modern textile mill and weaving cloth on a two harness loom in a small rural home. Above the table was a picture of a Japanese family wearing traditional Japanese clothing. A companion picture depicted a Japanese family in town wearing western-style clothing.

A large map of Japan was displayed on the floor. Near the map, there was a table displaying an opened atlas, a world globe, and a compass. Above the table, study prints depicting the topography of Japan were attractively arranged.

Near the map arrangement was a large table containing water colors, Japanese brushes, black ink, and pieces of rice paper. Above this arrangement were displayed a fine Japanese painting, a scroll of Japanese writing, and a Japanese blockprint by Hiroshegi.

A post for listening to recordings of Japanese music was available. Another listening post enabled children to listen to recordings of Japanese conversations. A third listening post enabled children to listen to translations of *haiku* poetry.

Two filmstrip viewers offering glimpses of the Japanese mode of living were placed nearby.

Motivated by the arranged environment which was rich in authentic materials, pictures, and artifacts reflecting the activities of people in Japan, the children expressed eagerness to explore, question, and identify themselves with the people of Japan.

ACTIVITY

After studying the pictures showing Japanese traditional dress, one boy dons the *obi* ("sash") and *zori* ("sandals"). In trying to identify with the Japanese father, he wanders into the home area showing his garb and talking as he thinks the Japanese father would. An opportunity to use the *shamoji* ("rice spatula") and the *ohitsu* ("wooden rice container") encourages one of the girls to feel she is a Japanese lady preparing food. The display of food from the nearby table provides the ingredients for the meal. Other children eagerly try to use the Japanese dishes and chopsticks, try their hand with the Japanese paint brushes, listen to the recordings at the various listening posts, or browse through the books and pictures on Japan.

The many questions that arise from this beginning awareness of life in Japan outlined the direction that the unit might take. The children's purposes were clearly defined through the questions they asked and the statements they made. "We need more dishes and chopsticks so we all can eat." "Is this all that the Japanese eat?" "How can they eat this?" "We need a table to put the dishes on." "What does the Japanese father do?" "Is it hard to learn to speak Japanese?" "Don't you have any more Japanese clothing?" Not all of the interests can be investigated at one time. Choices are made by the children in terms of which aspect of Japanese living would best further the progress of the group through the study and at the same time merit extensive investigation. On the basis of having used rice bowls, lacquer ware dishes, and chopsticks in the initial environment and during the subsequent dramatic situation, the group decided that their first major interest was in providing each member of the class with either chopsticks, rice bowls, saki cups, or lacquer ware dishes in order that all could participate realistically in being Japanese people whenever they were in the home setting. Thus, the first task for the total group was to find out about the nature of the items used in the preparation and consumption of food and the industrial arts processes involved in the making of chopsticks, rice bowls, saki cups, and lacquer ware. The children believed that any item they made would have to be authentic to Japanese culture, including the process, materials, and designs. Thus, inquiry into the nature of the food utensils was initiated.

The study and making of utensils contribute more than satisfying children's desires to be physically active, trying their success with new or different types of experiences, possessing personal items, accumulating information about Japanese culture, or realistically trying to get on the inside of the Japanese situation. Such outcomes are related primarily to pupil interests.

The teacher perceived that, while satisfying children's desires to know about Japanese culture, opportunity would occur for children to acquire techniques and strengthen skills of gathering data, classifying and organizing information, and synthesizing, generalizing, and hypothesizing on the information acquired. He perceived also that, through the children's interests in finding out more about Japanese houseware items, excellent opportunities existed for helping children understand significant ideas from various fields of knowledge.

DEVELOPING A GENERALIZATION FROM ANTHROPOLOGY

Knowing that children had been made aware of the importance of containers and cooking utensils for the preparation, preservation, storage, and eating of foods in their own home, the teacher knew that similar treatment of the same cultural category in a study of Japan could be useful to children in hypothesizing that man develops tools and techniques to aid his mode of living. Through noting that utensils and perhaps other tools are of use to many different peoples, children generalize that man develops tools and perhaps methods to aid his mode of living. As children investigate the mode of living in Japan, they ask the question: Do the people develop special tools or methods for communication, transportation, education, provision of food, clothing, shelter, and the like?

DEVELOPING A GENERALIZATION FROM CULTURAL GEOGRAPHY

Knowing that children would acquire information from a wide variety of sources to the effect that the Japanese converted the clay at their feet into bowls and cups of chinaware or porcelain, cut the bamboo from the fields to make chopsticks, processed the minerals from the soil of the village to produce colors and glazes for pottery and cloisonne, gathered the wood from nearby cypress trees and the sap from the sumac trees to produce beautiful and useful lacquer ware items, and drew their decorative designs from their observations of nature, the teacher realized that he must plan time for children to organize these examples of man's use of materials in ways which would enable pupils to note for themselves that man in Japan converts the materials of his geographic environment into useful forms to satisfy physical wants.

The task of evolving generalizations from related bits of information may be likened to a mathematical equation, i.e., $b + c + d + e + f + g = A^2$, in which A constitutes the generalization and the lower case letters comprise the unsystematic accumulation of related facts:

b, or Japanese convert clay from the local area into pottery (fact)

+c, or Japanese convert minerals from the local soil into colors and glazes (fact)

+d, or Japanese convert cypress wood from nearby trees into containers (fact)

+e, or Japanese convert bamboo from local fields into chopsticks (fact)

+f, or Japanese convert sumac sap from nearby trees into lacquer (fact)

_____
[2] A, or Japanese people convert materials of the local environment into utensils (generalization from cultural geography).

+g, or Japanese utilize local flora and fauna to create decorative design (fact).

Having evolved the generalization through inquiry into the category of utensils, the generalization may now become a hypothesis for inquiry into other important aspects of Japanese culture and into the pupils' own mode of living. In essence, the children have evolved a criterion for the study of cultures.

Identifying examples from learnings, acquired earlier during the study of home, community, and the state, which show that people in their own locale also reshape the materials of the geographic environment to fulfill needs, aid children in perceiving relatedness of the study of another culture to comprehending their own. When pupils recognize that they personally transform materials of their geographic environment to satisfy certain wants or needs, then the major generalization from cultural geography takes on meaning and the social studies program has interest for children.

DEVELOPING A GENERALIZATION FROM HISTORY

Through their inquiry into Japanese utensils, children can be helped to comprehend a major generalization from history: *The races, cultures, and civilizations in other areas of the world and of other historical periods have contributed to the growth of present civilization.*

As the time nears for children to consider the application of design to their utensil, examination is made of the available artifacts to identify characteristics of Japanese design. Children discuss and chart the varieties of designs noted on the artifacts, study prints, filmstrips, and other illustrations available to them in the textbooks and other reference sources. Accessible reading material on Japanese design is assimilated. A study trip to watch a Japanese potter at work contributes additional information.

Information gained from the variety of sources is sorted out, classified, and recharted into categories of traditional and contemporary design. During the process of reshaping the data, children identify similarities of present Japanese utensils with those made during earlier periods of Japanese civilization. Children note that—

1. Decorative designs on cups, bowls, and chopsticks are similar or identical with designs utilized by earlier generations.

2. Shapes of rice bowls, saki cups, and chopsticks are similar or identical with similar items from earlier periods of Japanese civilization.

3. Processes used today are similar or identical to those utilized by previous generations.

4. Materials used in the making of houseware items today are in many cases similar or identical with materials used by other generations of Japanese people.

It becomes apparent to many children that the design as well as shapes, materials, and processes of making cups, bowls, chopsticks, and other items used today by the Japanese show the influence of Japanese tradition.[3]

Children plan designs for their own item of construction, being careful to retain the characteristic elements of design which make Japanese objects unique. Throughout the investigation and creation of utensils, the teacher helps the children to note the similarities and differences among present and past utensils. When the activity is culminated, each child has a piece of pottery, lacquer ware, or set of chopsticks to use; and each has moved toward understanding that design, shape, materials, and processes used in making household items show the influence of Japanese tradition.

From the information that certain designs and uses of utensils had relevance to the role of religion in the lives of the people, the children are curious to know more about the religions of the Japanese.

On the basis of reading textbooks and supplementary books, study trips to a Buddhist temple and a Shinto shrine, discussions with a Buddhist priest, talking with an anthropologist from a nearby college, and viewing films, filmstrips,

---

[3] The same inference could be made had children elected first to gather data about shelter, diet, education, government, or another cultural category.

and study prints on religions in Japan, children acquire comprehensive information about the subject. Included in the information on religion were the following facts:

1. The very first Japanese people *(Ainu)* practiced the Shinto religion.
2. In the sixth century, the Chinese taught the Japanese about Buddhism.
3. Buddhism came from India to China and Korea.
4. Buddhism began in India 2,500 years ago.
5. Many people in Japan today believe in both Shinto and Buddhism.
6. At one time everyone in Japan had to believe in Shinto.
7. Today everyone is free to choose his religion.
8. There are also some Christians in Japan.

The relatedness of such facts to each other or to a major idea from the social sciences often remains unknown for children. Few children will realize that the set of facts has relevance to the generalization from history that other races, cultures, and civilizations in different areas of the world and historical periods have contributed to the growth of modern day civilization in Japan. However, providing opportunities for pupils to gather together the facts and to generalize from them makes possible comprehension of significant adult generalizations from various subject matter categories. Children are apt to lose track of particular facts inasmuch as they often are drawn from a variety of sources and acquired over an extended period of time. When the separate facts can be brought together during processes of organizing and classifying data through the use of charts, graphs, time lines, pictorial maps, paintings, murals, and stories, the relationships can be readily perceived and the inferences made; in this case, the religious practices of present Japanese civilization have been influenced by other Asian cultures. A similar revelation that architecture, diet, education, government, and other aspects of culture have been likewise influenced by other Asian nations could be derived from the pupils' further analyses of the Japanese mode of living.

Further study of the activities of the Japanese mode of living reveals other examples or "for instances" which reinforce the major generalization being developed.

JAPANESE CIVILIZATION SHOWS INFLUENCE OF OTHER ANCIENT ASIAN CULTURES

As children, through satisfying their desire to learn to speak and write a few Japanese words, find out that Japanese writing developed, in part, from Chinese writing; that Japanese speech patterns are similar to Chinese speech patterns; and that the Japanese language is similar to the Chinese and Korean languages, they are accumulating examples, or "for instances," which demonstrate that differing races, cultures, and civilizations contributed to the development of the current mode of living (language).

JAPANESE CIVILIZATION SHOWS INFLUENCE OF JAPANESE TRADITION

Children learn from a story read by the teacher that for a great many years Japanese families were often large. Grandparents, parents, brothers, and sisters often lived together with their families. Since the children wonder why traditional Japanese family life is so different from American family life, they realize the need to find out more about the sociological structure of Japan.

A local historian whose area of specialization is Asia is interviewed. Information available in the classroom library is gathered. A trip to a central public library provides additional materials for the study. From all of these sources, the children learn a primitive white people called *Ainu* lived on the islands thousands of years ago. Settlers came from Asia and gathered their families together in clans. Each clan was made up of one large family that ruled itself. With each clan there was a chief whom they believed to be a god. The clans often fought each other; and during the third and fourth centuries A.D., the Yamato clan became the leader.

As the children dramatize their learnings about clan life, past history takes on new meaning. When the emerging Yamato clan controlled the other clans, the children learn that powerful families became the real rulers of Japan. Although the emperor was thought of as a god, he did not actually rule. At times, a family of soldiers ruled; these rulers were called *shoguns*. When a *shogun* was in power, the government was called a *shogunate*. It was protected by warriors called *sumari*. These warriors taught Japanese boys that it was an honor to suffer or die as a soldier. From such information, children acquired additional examples illustrating that the Japanese beliefs and customs of today had their beginnings many years ago.

JAPANESE CIVILIZATION SHOWS INFLUENCE OF OTHER CURRENT CIVILIZATIONS

In reading about Japan in the newspapers and viewing programs about modern day Japan on television, the children become curious about the changes taking place in Japan. In pursuing the topic of change, they decide to visit a Japanese section of the city, continue reading current newspaper accounts of life in Japan, check television logs for informational programs about Japan, and read contemporary sources for additional information on the changing patterns of living in Japan.

From a study trip to the Japanese section and from the other sources investigated, the children learn that many traditional home industries have given way to industrialization. The ideas for industrialization have come from other parts of the world. They learn also that many Japanese no longer think of the emperor as a god since the traditional government has changed. As a result of foreign commerce, household items also have changed and include items not traditional in a Japanese home. The use of bicycles and automobiles by the Japanese for transportation seems to result from contact with other countries. Even the Japanese diet has changed somewhat; it now includes milk, cheese, and bread. From all this knowledge, the children seek to discern relatedness and in doing so arrive at the understanding that the Japanese civilization reflects other current civilizations.

As has been indicated previously, through the inquiry into the cultural category of utensils, the children learned that household utensils and social structure used in Japan today show the influence of Japanese tradition. In finding out about the cultural categories of religion, language, government, and family tradition, children move toward the concept that the present Japanese civilization reflects the influence of other ancient Asian cultures. In learning about industry, government, architecture, and daily living activities in Japan today, children perceive that modern civilization in Japan reflects the influence of other current civilizations. These three concepts add up to the major generalization from history: Other races, cultures, and civilizations in different areas of the world and historical periods have contributed to the evolution of modern day civilization in Japan. Through identifying corresponding analogies, examples, and "for instances" in other contrasting cultures including their own, certain children can be helped to generalize still further: Past and present civilizations represent our cultural heritage. The races, cultures, and civilizations in most areas of the world and of most historical periods, beginning with the dawn of recorded history, have made some contributions to the growth of our present civilizations.

It is through the inductive processes of acquiring and classifying examples of related learnings that the significant adult generalizations from categories of knowledge come to take on meaning for children. It is in the replicatory nature of concept development that understanding occurs and a relatedness of the social studies program to actual aspirations, interests, and concerns of mankind are recognized by children in the intermediate grades.

The task of helping pupils to perceive relatedness among the myriad of facts acquired in their activities in school to significant ideas, concepts, generalizations, and hypotheses influencing the modes of living in contrasting patterns of cultures is at best a complex task.

Understanding a pattern of culture requires a study of the essentials of societal life over and over in different situations, from various points of view, and from successively higher levels of understanding. One must strive to relate learnings to personal example, then set about purposely and consistently to lift the example to ever higher levels of abstraction. Perceiving the social studies as a continuum program from grades K-14, the inductive developing of generalizations over a long time period, replicating and practicing the strategies of learning of the social scientists, and examining significant societal situations from a variety of perspectives, all have implications for organizing the social studies such that the learning activities will be valued by children.

In this structure, children can be helped to acquire for themselves the major rules, laws, ideas, hypotheses, concepts, or generalizations not only from anthropology, cultural geography, and history but also from economics, sociology, political science, psychology, physical geography, philosophy, and other fields of knowledge. The inductive development of significant generalizations which govern our mode of living is a challenging and interesting emphasis for guiding instruction in the social studies curriculums of the intermediate grades today.

CONCLUSION

The foregoing chapters have presented a modern perspective for guiding pupils through learning experiences in the social studies. Based on the assumption that there are literally thousands of concepts and generalizations which must be acquired in order to understand and interpret one's physical and social world, considerable attention is directed toward the processes for developing concepts and generalizations from the social sciences. Special treatment is given to identifying the relatedness of factual information to the understandings of concepts and to broad generalizations. Perceiving relatedness among the myriad of facts accumulated by pupils to significant ideas which govern the activities of mankind is foundational in the structure of the social studies.

The importance of gaining insight into the processes for developing concepts and generalizations cannot be overestimated. David Russell notes that:

> More than anything else they [concepts] are the premises, the foundations, and the structural steel of thinking.[1]

In a recent study, *Fostering Intellectual Development in Young Children,* Wann, Dorn, and Liddle state that:

> A system of concepts provides the basis for efficient learning through reducing the complexity of the environment. . . . The formation and utilization of concepts represent one of the most basic forms of cognition by which man deals with his environment.[2]

The development of significant concepts and generalizations has as its basis the cultivation of the rational powers of each pupil. The development of the powers to recall and imagine, classify and generalize, analyze and synthesize, deduce and infer, and compare and evaluate leads to the development of the pupil's powers to perceive significant relationships, to achieve personal goals, and to contribute to the management of society. The importance of providing opportunities for pupils to acquire, develop, and practice the skills of inquiry, gather and classify data, and reshape knowledge better to serve the goals of the individual and society is stressed as essential in the structure of the modern social studies curriculums.

The acquisition of one's cultural heritage and the assumption of the proper role of a citizen is impossible without the intellectual means to study events, to relate one's values to them, and to make decisions based on knowledge of alternative actions and possible consequences of each. The Educational Policies Commission in *Central Purpose of American Education* notes the importance of developing one's rational powers in these terms:

---

[1] Russell, David. *Children's Thinking.* Boston: Ginn and Co., 1956. p. 122.

[2] Wann, Kenneth D.; Dorn, Miriam S.; and Liddle, Elizabeth A. *Fostering Intellectual Development in Young Children.* New York: Teachers College, Columbia University, 1962. p. 12.

A person with developed rational powers has the means to be aware of all facets of his existence. . . . He can escape captivity to his emotions and irrational states. He can enrich his emotional life and direct it toward ever higher standards of taste and enjoyment. He can enjoy the political and economic freedoms of the democratic society. He can free himself from the bondage of ignorance and unawareness. He can make of himself a free man.[3]

Organizing the social studies as a laboratory to study societies and cultures while striving to develop in pupils the skills to evolve criteria, extend inquiry, and reshape knowledge in a variety of ways gives the child the power to evolve the essential framework into which he can interpret information and experiences and thereby gain control over the factors that influence his mode of living and give shape to his aspirations.

The modern social studies program establishes an inductive approach for learning, not only for the acquisition of the ideas, rules, principles, laws, and hypotheses which represent the cultural heritage of civilization today but also for the provision of the means for the evolution of the different concepts, generalizations, and classifications of knowledge that are not yet revealed to mankind.

BIBLIOGRAPHY

California State Department of Education. *Report of the State Central Committee on Social Studies to the California State Curriculum Commission.* Sacramento: California State Department of Education, 1961.

Hanna, Paul R. "Structure of Knowledge: The Interrelationship of Ideas." *The Nature of Knowledge.* Milwaukee: Edward A. Uhrig Foundation, 1962.

Michaelis, John U. *Social Studies for Children in a Democracy.* Englewood Cliffs, N.J.: Prentice-Hall, 1963.

National Council for the Social Studies. *Skill Development in Social Studies.* Thirty-Third Yearbook. (Edited by Helen McCracken Carpenter.) Washington, D.C.: the Council, a department of the National Education Association, 1963.

National Council for the Social Studies, National Education Association. *Social Studies in Elementary Schools.* Thirty-Second Yearbook. (Edited by John U. Michaelis.) Menasha, Wis.: George Banta Co., 1962.

National Education Association, Educational Policies Commission. *The Central Purpose of American Education.* Washington, D.C.: the Commission, 1961.

Postman, Leo. "Recent Developments in the Experimental Analysis of Learning and Concept Formation." *New Dimensions in Learning.* Washington, D.C.: Association for Supervision and Curriculum Development, a department of the National Education Association, 1962.

U.S. Department of Health, Education, and Welfare, Office of Education. *Implications for Elementary Education: Followup on the 1960 White House Conference on Children and Youth.* Washington, D.C.: Government Printing Office, 1961.

Wann, Kenneth D.; Dorn, Miriam S.; and Liddle, Elizabeth A. *Fostering Intellectual Development in Young Children.* New York: Teachers College, Columbia University, 1962.

---

[3] National Education Association, Educational Policies Commission. *The Central Purpose of American Education.* Washington, D.C.: the Commission, 1961. pp. 8-9.

Date Due